HOW TO
THEY/THEM

A VISUAL GUIDE TO
Nonbinary Pronouns and the
World of Gender Fluidity

Stuart Getty

Illustrated by Brooke Thyng

SASQUATCH BOOKS

SEATTLE

Printed in China

SASQUATCH BOOKS with colophon is a registered trademark of Penguin Random House LLC

26 25 24 23 22   9 8 7 6 5 4 3

Editor: Hannah Elnan
Production editor: Bridget Sweet
Designer: Alicia Terry
Illustrations: Brooke Thyng

Library of Congress Cataloging-in-Publication Data
Names: Getty, Stuart, author. | Thyng, Brooke, illustrator.
Title: How to they/them : a visual guide to nonbinary pronouns and the
world of gender fluidity / Stuart Getty ; illustrations, Brooke Thyng.
Description: Seattle : Sasquatch Books, [2020]
Identifiers: LCCN 2020018220 (print) | LCCN 2020018221 (ebook) | ISBN
9781632173133 (hardcover) | ISBN 9781632173140 (ebook)
Subjects: LCSH: Grammar, Comparative and general–Pronoun.
Classification: LCC P279 .G48 2020 (print) | LCC P279 (ebook) | DDC
425/.55–dc23
LC record available at https://lccn.loc.gov/2020018220
LC ebook record available at https://lccn.loc.gov/2020018221

ISBN: 978-1-63217-313-3

Sasquatch Books
1325 Fourth Avenue, Suite 1025
Seattle, WA 98101

SasquatchBooks.com

Dedicated to the number 17

Contents

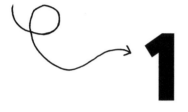

1 Binaries on Binaries   53

2 "But It's Grammatically Incorrect!": Language, Other Tips, and Facts   101

3

The Fun Stuff (and Some Not-Fun Stuff) 175

Preface:
How to They

They it good:

Gently place your tongue against the inside of your front two teeth.

Now blow until a whistling *th* sound lightly emerges.

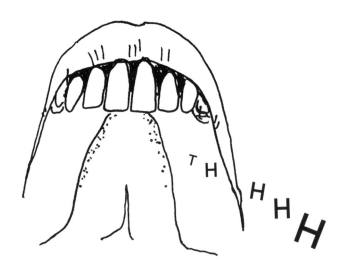

(*They* it, don't spray it.)

Now, open the mouth to say *ey*, as in the letter *A* or the sound Canadians make at the end of sentences, kinda.

Or like a friend is driving by in a car and you want to get their attention.

Try it together now:

-EY

It's literally that easy. For your mouth.
But your brain—well, that's a little harder.

Don't worry. I got you.

Intro:
The Story of Stuart

Hi. I'm Stuart.

I was born in Louisville, Kentucky: Katherine Stuart Getty.

Kentucky is known for horses, good bourbon, and fried chicken—

not gay stuff.

(But boy, was I gay.)

It was in me all along.

The feeling of being not quite female, not quite male . . . not quite like "the other girls."

Growing up in Kentucky, I was a tomboy. A weird little kid.

Think bowl cut, buckteeth, skinned knees. Tomboy was this "OK" category for girls who liked to do boy things and wear boy clothes.

Maybe there was a touch of shame or guilt to it, to not be what a "female" should be? Being a tomboy was second tier, almost—*like* a girl, but not the best kind of girl.

I was good at sports. I lettered and won rings. *Tomboy.*

It gave me a free pass from wearing dresses and frilly things mostly, except to church and some fancy dinners, and every time, I would cry and refuse and throw my Sam & Libbys at the door. Usually I lost the fight and ended up tearstained, hiding wrecked knees under itchy white tights. Ugh, those tights. Laura Ashley. Paisleys. Headbands with bows on them. All of it—just no.

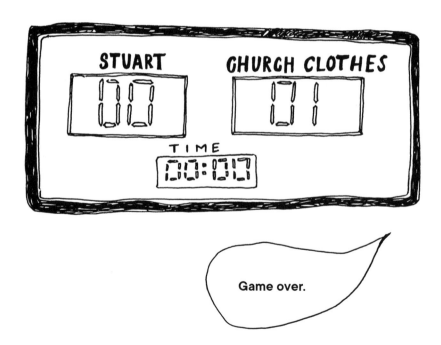

Game over.

Growing up, I'd get,

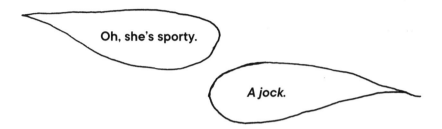

Oh, she's sporty.

A jock.

The words we carry craft who we become. I think it helped me, maybe, to just start out living outside of the stereotypical gendered norms. Like how I dressed. How I spoke. How I wrestled with my brother. Perhaps I was even louder and more of a class clown because I got to step outside of what a little girl was supposed to be.

Perhaps *tomboy* was my first taste of

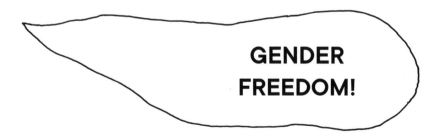

GENDER FREEDOM!

I'm thankful for my tomboy moment and my softball life (*so many years of softball*) and also my time at Camp Piomingo, where I saw women with armpit and leg hair . . . and happy trails!

Young, feminist counselors just lezzing out in the middle of the forest—it was revolutionary for me, so freeing. So formative. They were so cool with their tie-dye and Birkenstocks. Which, interestingly enough, is basically all I wear now.

These are my roots.
My happy trails.

It started with the name Stuart,
and that's what changed first.

(Well, I mean, before that,

I started kissing girls,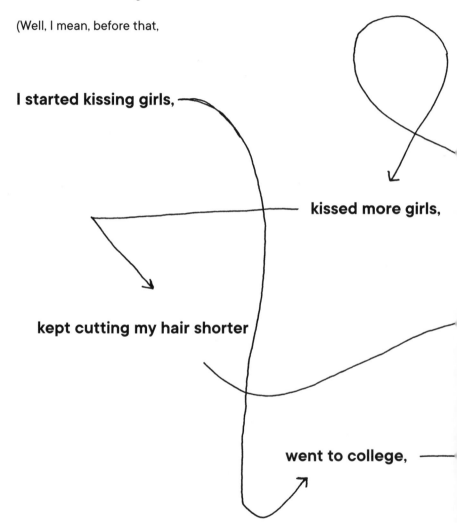

kissed more girls,

kept cutting my hair shorter

went to college,

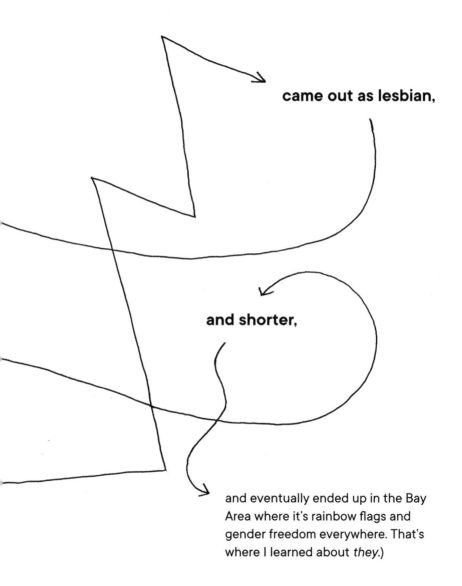

came out as lesbian,

and shorter,

and eventually ended up in the Bay Area where it's rainbow flags and gender freedom everywhere. That's where I learned about *they*.)

Before I asked for a new pronoun, I found Stuart.

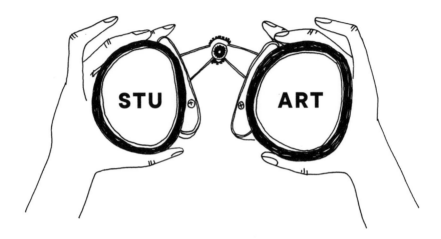

I didn't have to look that far, really. It's my middle name.

My mom, sister, and brother all have Stuart as their middle name too.

It's my mom's maiden name.

So it works for me.

Stuart is in the middle.

At that time, I was taking a lot of Lyfts for work. The drivers would roll up and spot me, then hesitate, seeing the name Kate on their screen. They'd give me this look, like,

Wait, you're a sir,

you're . . .

not . . .

Kate.

Nope. I'm not.

(See. It was there all along.)

At first, it was only in some circles. Just queer friends.

I used Kate at work still—with family too.

Like a mullet:

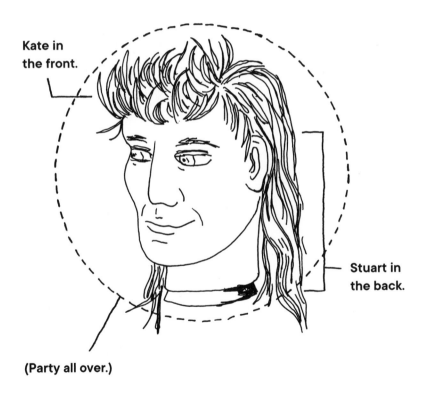

Kate in the front.

Stuart in the back.

(Party all over.)

The more I grew into knowing myself. the less I used Kate.

And *she* and *her* too.

(Especially coupled with Stuart.

She's Stuart?

lol.)

So, how'd I start using it?

It being the pronoun *they*.

I learned about *they* at a queer spiritual gathering in the woods. A few others asked for it in a pronoun circle. A **pronoun circle** is when people meet and while sharing their names, they share their pronouns too. It's so everyone is on the same page; it gives everyone a chance to affirm their own gender—and to add any other important tidbits that might help people get to know them and avoid assuming anything.

Like this:

It was after seeing many others doing it, using this **weird*** pronoun, that I thought, *Hmm, could I be this thing too?*

*To clarify, I use the word **weird** with love. I wear it as a badge of pride. And I say *weird* pronoun with love because, god bless it, sometimes the singular *they* can be a real pain in the rear.

(Ouch.)

I say **weird** pronoun because maybe it does make people feel weird at first. Even when I first started asking for it . . .

It felt **we¡r d.**

Funny.

But weird is OK.

Weird is good.

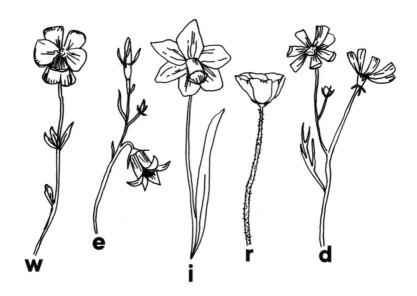

Weird means growth is happening.

Weird is what pushes us to our edges so we can stretch and grow and be more.

Weird is every future new thing that doesn't exist yet.

Weird is the way.

Looking back, it was because I found *weird* and amazing communities that held me in such openness and freedom that I was able to find my truths.

And that's my wish for everyone.

I really hope that this book can be that too:

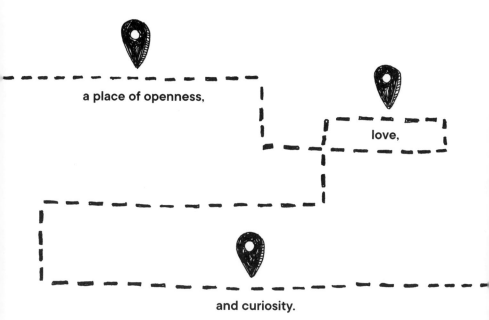

a place of openness,

love,

and curiosity.

A place to learn . . . a place where you're offered acceptance and understanding.

A place to talk openly about this thing so many people find so confusing . . . a place to have your burning questions answered.

But more than that, I hope this book is a place of hope.

I hope we all dream to find
our own realities.

Even if those realities
don't even exist yet.

Especially if they don't.

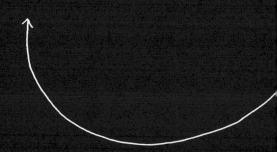

I hope we can create a new world where everyone—no matter their
pronoun, identity, or sexual orientation—can be free to explore
being exactly the person they want to be.

Because that's what this is all about.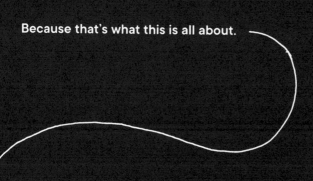

This is more than just pronouns and grammar lessons and arguments about bathrooms—this is about freedom of expression and the *human* right to choose for one's self how to identify one's self.

And while *they* might only be for some, that freedom* is for everyone.

*You just have to grab it. Let's.

They 101

Before we dig in, let's get some basics under our belts.

Q:

Why does *they* exist?

A:

The pronoun *they* exists because binary gender terms (a.k.a. man and woman) are too limiting for the myriad identities people want to express. Language has evolved to meet the needs of people. *They* is how some people feel seen as beyond the gender identities of man and woman. *They* is a gender-free pronoun.

For me, *they* exists because I needed it to. I didn't fit otherwise. *They* existing is like this breath of fresh air every time I don't have to hear "Sir" or "Thanks, ladies." Like I don't have to fit into those two boxes. Like taking off my shoes after a long day.

Ahhhhh.

They exists because the queer collective, and humans in general, tried other words for a nonbinary gender pronoun—and they just didn't stick. Some of those other pronouns:

Ou: Genderless pronoun from 1808. Now extinct.

Co: Coined by feminist writer Mary Orovan in 1970. Still used, especially in communities where people are *co*-living.

The most-used neutral pronouns are:

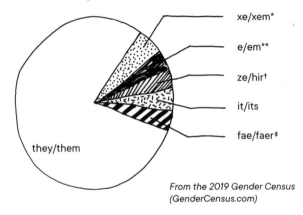

- xe/xem*
- e/em**
- ze/hir†
- it/its
- fae/faer‡

they/them

From the 2019 Gender Census (GenderCensus.com)

*Xe/Xem: Apparently invented by a bunch of people. Still around. Pronounced *xee*, like whistling your *Z*, or like *ksee*.

**E/Em, Ey/Em: Most popularly known as "the Spivak pronouns." Used in online communities. Big in the '80s. Still used online. Pronounced *hee*, or like *they* minus the *th* part.

†Ze/Hir, Ze/Zir: The most widely known gender-neutral pronouns besides *they*. (*Ze* is pronounced with the hard *e*: *zee*.) Big in the '80s and '90s. Still seen but rare.

‡Fae/Faer: You guessed it, used by faerie-identifying people. (It's a spiritual path.)

P.S. I love *fae/faer*.

While people mostly use *they* the way we all learned to on gram-mar chalkboards (as a plural), we also use *they* to indicate one person when we don't know their gender. And we do it without even realizing it.

Wow, our brains.

I bet you do it for your mail carrier:

Did they bring my package yet?

See, it's in your brain too. So when the world craved a gender-neutral pronoun, *they* just stayed.

I am betting more words will exist in the future to encompass this identity. And all the other identities we haven't even discovered yet.

They is just what we're doing right now—and by *we*, I mean Westerners, and maybe even more specifically, people living on the coasts in the United States and in more liberal pockets across the English-speaking world.

But, what's next?

Who knows? You tell me.

PRIORITY MAIL

Q:

What does *they* mean?

A:

Someone using *they* suggests that using *she* or *he* doesn't feel right. It usually means that person doesn't feel like a man or a woman and thinks of gender as more expansive and fluid. But the goal of it all (the whole *they* thing, and all gender expression, really) is to let everyone find who they are and do whatever they want to honor that identity. The freedom to wear what they want, speak how they want, be whatever feels right.

That's *they*'s mission: more freedom for everyone.

So, yes, usually if someone is using the *they* pronoun, they are trying to tell you their gender is not man or woman.

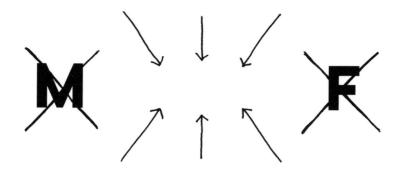

But just ask. Because every person's story is different.

So many of us just want to be asked our story.

(What's yours?)

Q:

Where did *they* come from?

A:

The singular *they* arose in the English language as a response to the need for more than just *he* or *she*.

 Only a third of the world's languages include gendered pronouns. In other languages, they have different pronouns for *me, you, some other person*; or in other places, pronouns are classifications that don't have to do with gender at all but instead signify honor, rank, social roles, etc.

To *they* or not to *they*?

The singular *they* can be found as early as 1375 in English writing. Shakespeare dabbled in some *they* play. Emily Dickinson too. *He* has also been proposed as a pronoun for everyone, but generation after generation, that just kept pissing people off.

THEY.

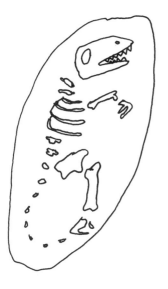

Outside of Western culture, there is evidence that gender-neutral or "third gender" identities have existed pretty much since the beginning of most civilizations. So, the underlying concept behind *they* didn't really come from one place or time. The need for this nonbinary identity has been everywhere, always.

Q:

Who can use *they*?

A:

Trick question! Anyone can.

(People who use *they* look all the different types of ways.)

Q:

Why do people say they dislike *they*?

A:

1. "I learned different grammar than that."

2. "I don't get it."

3. "I'm regressive in my view of gender roles for men and women. Toxic masculinity is fine by me. Women should be in the kitchen. Therefore, the rigidity of *M* and *F* is safe to me. Any disturbance to this binary is not welcome. And I usually wear a red hat."*

4. "But . . . it's *plural*." (That's just number one again, but stubborn about it.)

*Love is the future. Not hatred.

1. It's like learning a new language. True, you'll have to tweak that "*they* is always plural" grammar rule you've learned, but many dictionaries and style guides have taken the singular *they* into their loving arms. Language is constantly evolving. Are you?

2. It takes some initial effort, but it's possible. And it's worth it to help friends feel safe and understood.

3. I only hope the best for you. But I do honestly think a reckoning is coming for this type of thinking.

4. See number one. Or, you know, keep reading this book.

Q:

Why is it important to bring pronouns into spaces if everyone's using binary pronouns (*he* or *she*)?

A:

It's important because, above all, no assumptions. Don't just look around a room and assume by looking at clothing, hair, and mannerisms, *OK, got their genders*. That's gender-clocking. And there might be someone there who could surprise you.

Instead, get in the practice of allowing everyone to tell you for themselves how they want to be seen and referred to. If people started making pronoun talk comfy in all spaces, *they*-using friends like me wouldn't always have to be the one bringing it up. And, tbh, that makes us all feel safer.

But wait . . . have we gotten ahead of ourselves? We need to break this all.

The.

Way.

Down.

What's a *binary*?

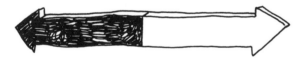

A **binary** is something having two parts, usually illustrated as a spectrum with "opposites" on each end. Like: black and white, right and wrong, gay and straight.

Fluid spectrums, or binaries, have been good ways to describe *they* and the concepts that help define it.

Part One:
Binaries on Binaries

The Big Three

Let's start with the basics. When trying to understand all of this—*this* being *they* and really just gender and identity in general—there are essentially three big concepts to, you know,

Get It

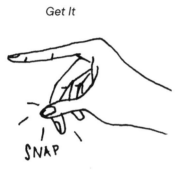 

SNAP

SNAP

with a capital G:

1. **Sex Assigned at Birth (SAAB)** (Not to be confused with Saabs—cool cars, especially the convertibles)

2. **Gender Identity (+)**

3. **Sexual Orientation**

So, let's do this. Let's go on this journey together.

First up,

1. Sex Assigned at Birth (SAAB)

When you're born and they look at your physical body and then say,

It's a girl.

It's a boy.

Congrats! It's a *they*!

What we used to think was the only thing going on:

Sex:

Male	Female
Peen	Vag
Testicles	Ovaries
Testosterone	Estrogen
Chromosomes	Chromosomes
XY	**XX**

Stuart was assigned female at
birth (AFAB).

My brothers: AMAB.

How FAB.

"Sex" is just a box we put people into. It starts with doctors looking at your junk at birth, and then, as a society, we roll with it from there.

Sex: The categories (male, female, intersex, etc.) into which humans are divided on the basis of their reproductive functions.

Though this is the technical, medical definition of "biological sex," it's not so simple.

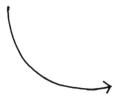

What's also going on:

<u>Sex:</u>

External anatomy can look a bunch of different ways.

So can internal anatomy.

So can hormones.

So can chromosomes.

XX

XY

XØ*

XXY*

XXXY*

XYXY*

*These are examples of **intersex** classifications, which means having sexual characteristics outside the binary norm. Though it might seem rare, one in fifteen hundred individuals is born intersex. (That's about the same percentage of people in the world who have red hair. Shout out to my intersex friends with red hair. You're really doing something special!)

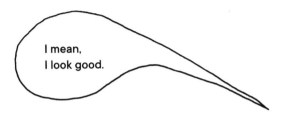

Original life on earth was
a blend of all sexes and
could reproduce with itself,
so there's that.

Bodies are all over the place chromosomally, hormonally, and biologically.

Like . . .

Sex Chromosomes: They are what determines our sex, and we are taught in school that females have two X chromosomes, males have an X and a Y, and that's that.

That can be the truth, sure.

But other variations exist:

→ People with Klinefelter's syndrome have three sex chromosomes: XXY. They are generally AMAB but can have some differences in their sex organs, hormones, and other physical developments.

→ Those with Turner's syndrome are AFAB, born partly or completely missing an X chromosome. So *XØ* marks the spot for them.

→ Sometimes humans and animals can also have two sets of chromosomes, like XXXY, XYXY, and so on.

→ *Gossip Girl's* chromosomes: XOXO

Hormones: We all think of **testosterone** as the "male hormone," and more testosterone means more manliness and, you know, big trucks, chest hair, and shirt vests . . .

But all people make testosterone.

The ways hormones show up in bodies can vary greatly, no matter what SAAB you're rocking.

High estrogen levels in AFAB people can actually show up as body hair, bursts of anger, and other attributes most commonly associated with high testosterone levels.

Science, and the lived experience of humans around the world, shows us that bodies are more fluid than the rigid classifications of "biological sex."

So if we limit ourselves to this binary classification, just look how many people we leave out. Wild, huh?

What's beautiful is: when we realize so many different types of people and bodies do exist, we stop considering "male" and "female" to be *normal*. **Allowing for a wider diversity of humans and life experiences lets people define for themselves what *normal* means.** Being intersex or having different abilities and needs . . . these aren't things that need to be fixed, or indicators of "something wrong."

These are parts of valid and beautiful humans who also deserve love and acceptance in this world.

Or at least the world I'm hoping we all want to create together.

2. Gender Identity (+)

Gender Identity

A.k.a. one's own sense of self in terms of gender.

Identity is how you see yourself.

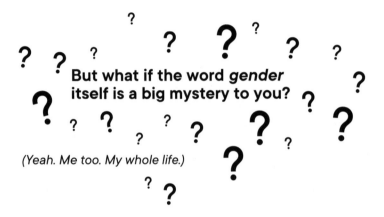

But what if the word *gender* itself is a big mystery to you?

(Yeah. Me too. My whole life.)

Gender: The behavioral, cultural, or psychological traits typically associated with one sex.

So, wait,

what's the difference between *gender* and *sex?*

Before modern times, the words *gender* and *sex* meant the same thing and there were only two options (*M* and *F*). But as research has evolved, so has this concept.

Gender is no longer seen as only two points on a line but, to many, as a fluid spectrum.

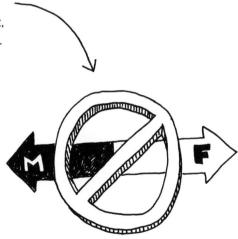

Like this:

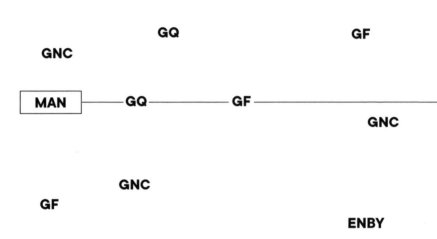

GQ

GF

GNC

| MAN |——— GQ ——————— GF ————————————

GNC

GNC

GF

ENBY

ENBY*: Nonbinary
GNC: Gender nonconforming
GQ: Genderqueer
GF: Genderfluid

*We use the spelling *enby* for nonbinary because
NB means "non-Black" in some circles.

The **gender binary** is the classification of gender on a spectrum from man to woman.

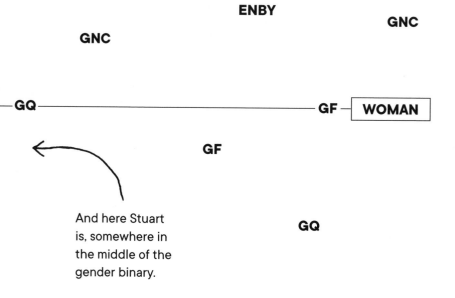

And here Stuart is, somewhere in the middle of the gender binary.

Some believe gender to be a spectrum with infinite shades in between . . . That's where *they* comes in.

(And the color gray, hybrid vehicles, turducken, you get it.)

Still others believe gender is beyond a linear definition—and laugh at the entire construct of using a binary for it, even challenging the belief that man and woman are "opposites."

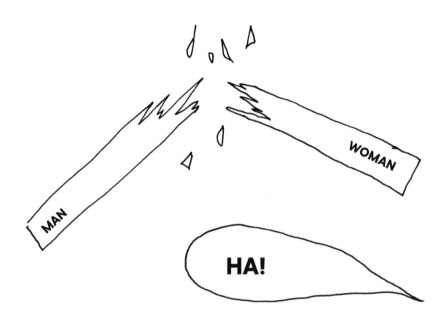

That's why *they* is described as both *between* and *beyond*.

Gender identity is your *own* sense of your *own* gender.

I feel like italics are warranted here because it's important for me, as someone who identifies as genderqueer—a gender identity different than most—to know that

the freedom is out there for me to choose for my *own* self and *own* that truth every day.

Gender identity is about feeling your body, knowing what's right, and following your *own* guidance. This doesn't just apply to gender-neutral folks; this means being a woman however you want to be a woman and being a man however you want to be a man. This means not letting anyone else tell you how to do you. (You know, unless that's your *thing*.)

The term *gender identity* was minted in the '60s as a way to disagree with the school of thought that believed gender was linked only to biology (a.k.a. sex assigned at birth).

There's a hot debate about where gender identity really comes from—not the word but, like, in us humans.

Are we born with our gender identity or is it socialized? Is it nature or nurture? What part is genetics? Much of this is still a shrug because studies say it's a mix of all of these things.

Hormones

Genetics

Born with it

Nature

Socialization

Nurture

Brain disposition

When you start to research gender identity, everything is phrased like, "it may affect" or "could be attributed to." But there is evidence in some people (see, now I'm doing it) that genetics, brain disposition, and hormones all affect gender identity. But these biological truths may also affect different people differently, and to differing degrees. Every single body is a unique cocktail of all the things in it (i.e., nature) mixed with socialization (i.e., nurture).

So that hot debate, well, can just cool it.

Gender reveal parties (for a fetus) do not actually reveal gender.
Instead, they're like a junk alert or an anatomy announcement! All you
know at that point, really, is the type of genitals your kid will (probably) be born with. What that means in terms of their gender (and even
sex, as we're finding out) is TBD.

Did you know that some people find the concept of gender reveals to
be transphobic? Because the concept of linking sex organs to gender
means eliminating the freedom to express one's own gender. (And
thus erasing trans people.)

My child has a penis . . . their gender
is TBD, check back in a few years.
Enjoy the cake and our
gray-scale color scheme.

Our gender expression is how we act and show up in the world.

Basically: if we prefer ties or dresses or both,

the words we choose,

how we move our hands when we speak,

maybe even our handwriting.

All the things that make a person a person.

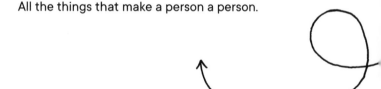

Gender expression is what someone expresses to the world: a person's behavior, mannerisms, interests, and appearance associated with gender, like femininity, masculinity, and any shade or mixture between or beyond the two. This also includes gender roles.

Q:

Is gender expression the same as gender identity?

A:

Not quite. Typically, yes, they do match. But that's not always the case. And it's a privilege to live the gender outside (expression) that you feel on the inside (identity).

What I mean is that some things are easier to control when expressing our identity. Some people have more freedom than others. Some people may never live a life where they feel safe enough to externally express the gender they feel inside. Some people won't have enough money for electrolysis or plastic surgery or hormones that could allow them to achieve the gender expression that aligns with their gender identity.

So, yeah, it's a privilege.

Some other ways people who use *they* identify:

Nonbinary means to exist outside the traditional gender binary of man to woman. Some nonbinary people think of themselves in the middle, some outside the spectrum altogether. Some not even on the same page as the binary drawn. Some in another room altogether.

Some prefer the terms **gender neutral** or **gender nonconforming** instead of nonbinary because of the belief that using the word *binary* reinforces its existence, something we're trying to rethink or maybe ctrl+alt+delete.

Androgynous usually means that, externally, you live in a very "Wait, is that a boy or a girl?" space and are probably very comfortable there.

Gender nonconforming, or **GNC**, means that a person's behaviors and gender expression do not match masculine or feminine gender norms (e.g., gender variant, gender diverse, gender atypical, gender creative).

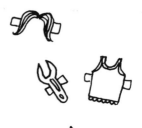

Genderfluid means that someone identifies as gender neutral, but the word *fluid* might also mean they identify as a woman some days, a man others, and genderqueer other days. It's flexible, evolving, and may exist on a plane beyond binaries as well.

Genderqueer means a person does not subscribe to conventional gender distinctions but identifies with neither, both, a blend of genders, or something in the beyond. Basically *queering up the concept of gender.*

(I love queering up everything we can. It's the gay agenda.)

Gender Identity (+)

OK, now that you understand gender identity, let's go a little deeper.

Fact:

Cisgender and transgender people exist in this world.

Transgender means that a person's gender identity doesn't match their SAAB. *Trans*, in Latin, means "across from" or "on the other side of"—on the other side of the gender you want, kinda. *Transgender* is also often used as an umbrella term to encompass all forms of gender nonconformity within the queer community. *They* is part of this crew. Holler.

Try this:

AFAB + Male Gender ID =

AFAB + Enby Gender ID* =

AMAB + Female Gender ID =

AMAB + Enby Gender ID* =

Yay, I'm trans!

*Yep, trans too!

Cis, short for **cisgender**, means a person's SAAB lines up with their gender identity. Or "your downstairs parts at birth match your gender identity." Some people think cis is an insult or something, but really, it's just Latin for "on this side of." (And the opposite of trans.)

Try this:

AFAB + Female Gender ID =

AMAB + Male Gender ID =

Yay, I'm cis!

Fact: Cis and transgender identities exist on a spectrum.

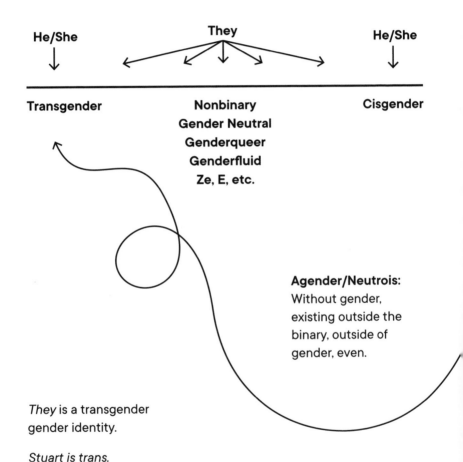

He/She

They

He/She

Transgender

Nonbinary
Gender Neutral
Genderqueer
Genderfluid
Ze, E, etc.

Cisgender

Agender/Neutrois:
Without gender,
existing outside the
binary, outside of
gender, even.

They is a transgender
gender identity.

Stuart is trans.

Yeehaw.

Fact: Transgender experiences also exist on a spectrum (and beyond).

(That's the plus part.)

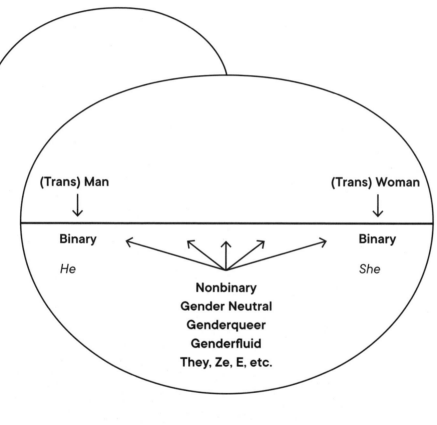

(Trans) Man

Binary

He

(Trans) Woman

Binary

She

**Nonbinary
Gender Neutral
Genderqueer
Genderfluid
They, Ze, E, etc.**

(A binary within a binary.

Wow. Life is cool.)

So, to review:

Hi, I'm Stuart, a transgender genderqueer person from Kentucky.

Notice I didn't say *transgendered*, because that word is awful and hurts trans people when they hear it. It sounds like my gender is being enacted upon me or something, instead of it being my actual identity. I read somewhere, "I wouldn't say I'm an Italian-ed American"—and *transgendered* is the same thing. It's not past tense; it's not like something happened and then you became something. A trans person is whatever they say they are, in all tenses—before, after, and during transition—and even if they never technically do the things we think about when we hear *transition*.

That "-ed" also puts such a focus on surgery, or the big transition, and many transgender people might not ever get surgery or transition and still identify as trans. Surgery is an elitist measure of trans-ness, and that "-ed" has no place in modern queer culture.

(OK, rant over. Thank you for coming to my talk.)

It's pretty rude to ask someone about their genitals. Trans or cis, weird looking or not. It's funny and sad that I have to say this, but it's like those warnings on plastic bags: *This is not a toy, don't put it over your head and breathe in deeply . . .* The warning is there . . . because people do it.

All

      the

           time.

                So . . . ———

(Rant over, for real now.)

A psychiatrist in 1965 coined the word **transgender**, claiming earlier terms were misleading.

(And they were. People lumped everything "trans-" together, including transvestites, or cross-dressers, a term that has nothing to do with gender identity. Most cross-dressers are straight cis men who dress up for kicks. So, no, not the same thing at all. The word *transgender* was needed. And *owned*.)

Since the 1990s, the term **transsexual** has been used to describe a subset of transgender people who desire to transition permanently—that is, those with the privilege to go do something about this desire, usually with the help of hormone therapy and surgery.

Terms like **trans man** and **trans woman** also exist to help people identify, if they like, with their trans-ness. Some like to flag it. Other people, after they transition, just want to be called a man or a woman, no trans about it.

Just a reminder that it's never OK to call someone "a transgender."
Instead, please say "transgender man" or "transgender woman"
or just "woman" or "man." And remember, some trans people are
neither man nor woman. They can be genderqueer, like me.
They is a trans identity too.

3. Sexual Orientation

A.k.a. your sexuality.

A.k.a. who gets your engine running.

A.k.a. who you're attracted to.

 **Asexual:** without sexual attraction.

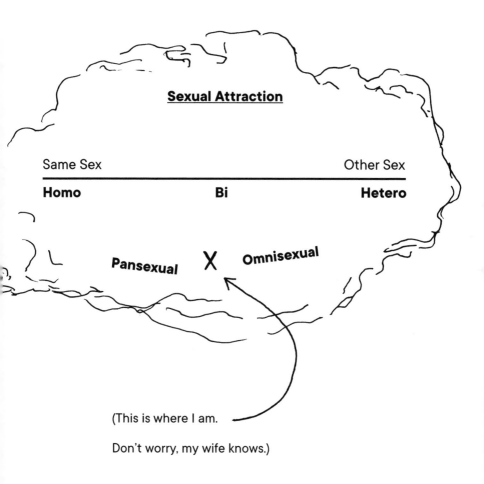

Sexual Attraction

Same Sex   Other Sex

Homo   **Bi**   **Hetero**

Pansexual   X   Omnisexual

(This is where I am.

Don't worry, my wife knows.)

A-Z
DICTIONARY

The term **omnisexual** reframes what many think of as "bisexuality" outside of the binary. It means "attracted to all genders." Like an omnivore, they eat all the things. *Zing.*

Pansexual is a similar term, meaning "gender blind" in sexual attraction.

Bisexual might be defined to some as "loving both genders," and thus, along a binary, however, many people say their "bi" means "attracted to all" and also don't assign a binary to their attractions.

Freedom is free.

OVIRAPTOR

Q:

So . . . what does *they/them* have to do with defining a person's sexuality, if anything?

A:

Basically, you're asking, is *they* gay? (I actually get this a lot.) And the answer is no. And yes. And sometimes. But technically speaking:

They is a gender identity, not a sexual orientaysh.

Remember:

Gender identity is your personal sense of gender along the spectrum of feminine to masculine, or beyond that spectrum. It's what feels right for you.

And *gay* is a sexuality.

Sexuality is who you like to do romantic and (most often) sexual things with, to, near, under, over, etc.

Yes, *they* can be *so* gay.

But it doesn't have to be . . .

Homosexuality means "loving the same sex."

It'd be up to the person using *they* to tell you who they like to get down with. And honestly, it's up to them to define their attractions as gay or not gay or gay-ish . . . not anyone else.

I suggest getting to know someone first before asking who they do sexual things with . . . but, you know, I was raised Kentucky polite.

I identify as a genderqueer in a lesbian relationship (gay marriage, technically) with a cis homosexual woman. Even as someone "not female-identifying anymore," that feels the most right. Categorizing relationships is a they-by-they basis.

But we do puzzles and scissor. So yes, this *they* is in something *gay*.

OK, so how do you feel? That was a lot of words and concepts and binaries.

And hopefully some

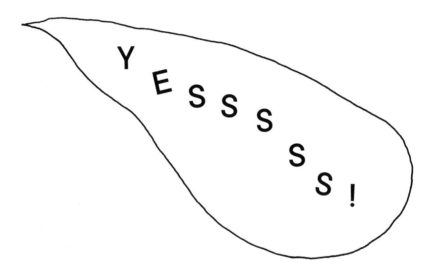

Y E S S S S S !

in there too.

Think of your own identity and where you fall on (or outside of) all of these binaries. Remember, it's up to you to decide. Nobody else gets to tell you how you do you. Or who to do. Ahem.

How do you identify?

M ——————————————————————————————— F

MAN ————————————————————————————— WOMAN

MASC ———————————————————————————— FEMME

TRANS ——————————————————————————— CIS

GAY —————————————————————————————— STRAIGHT

HOT —————————————————————————————— COOL

————————————————————————————————————

Part Two:
"But It's Grammatically Incorrect!"

Language, Other Tips, and Facts

Stop, Grammar Time

That's usually the first thing people ask about *they*: "But what about the grammar?!?"

It's true. When we learn English, we brain-pathway this chart:

Personal Pronouns

	Singular	Plural
First Person	I	We
Second Person	You	You All
Third Person	He, She, It	**They**

This chart is in there, muscle-memoried into everyday speech; you're at the grocery store, conjugating without even thinking. And as part of that conjugation, you're making a split-second decision about what someone's gender identity is, preparing to pull out a *he* or a *she*. What assumptions are you making? How do you know?

When you first start using *they* (as a singular pronoun for someone), you might always have to be thinking a little bit, or trying a little, at first, until it also becomes muscle-memoried as part of your brain and heart and soul. And it can.

It just takes practice. Don't worry, you got this.

You might be wondering,

How do I relearn something so deeply ingrained in my grammar-learned gray matter?

Step One: Acknowledge your grammar lessons and the neural pathways present in your brain. I literally visualize my brain's little sidewalks. I picture myself thanking them for their service.

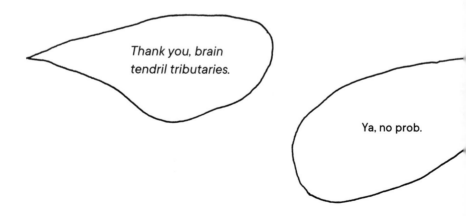

Thank you, brain tendril tributaries.

Ya, no prob.

Many times in your life, everything will line up to that grammar chart you've learned, and you'll get to use the same *they* neural pathway you always have.

Just because some people use *they* as singular doesn't mean its plural usage ceases to exist. (I know, I know. But I was recently asked this.)

Step Two: Acknowledge that many nonbinary folks want to use the singular *they*. By accepting this, a re-chart is in order:

Personal Pronouns

	Singular	Plural
First Person	I	We
Second Person	You	You All
Third Person	He, She, It, **They**	They

***Themself:** When people want a reflexive pronoun to go with the singular *they, themself* has arisen as an obvious choice, although autocorrect doesn't acknowledge it just yet. (Interestingly enough, the word *themselves* did not exist until the mid–1400s. In the late 1300s, *themself* was the default.)

Reflexive

	Singular	Plural
First Person	Myself	Ourselves
Second Person	Yourself	Yourselves
Third Person	Himself, Herself, Itself, **Themself***	Themselves

Possessive

	Singular	Plural
First Person	Mine	Ours
Second Person	Yours	Yours
Third Person	His, Hers, Its, **Theirs**	Theirs

Conjugation: Let's try it with a verb!

Personal Pronouns

	Singular	Plural
First Person	**I** rollerblade.	**We** rollerblade.
Second Person	**You** roller-blade.	**You** all rollerblade.
Third Person	Doc shreds; **he** rollerblades. Hilary shreds; **she** rollerblades. Stuart is a shredder; **they** rollerblade.* **It** is a fun time.	Stuart and their wife skate together. **They** rollerblade.

*You'll notice I conjugate the singular *they* like I do the plural *they*: "they rollerblade," no *s*. Sure, it's not how the rest of the grammar chart goes, but that's the point. *They* is changing the game. Like a rebel. Because it just sounds better and feels most natural without the *s*. And really, it's that simple.

Q:

What is a graceful way to clarify that you are using a singular *they* and not a plural *they* when talking about someone who uses *they* pronouns?

A:

Context clues. That's what I do. I just say a few more words with my mouth to let the person I'm talking to know I'm referring to one person with my *they*s.

How to Use Context Clues

A great on-ramp to pronoun town is avoiding pronouns altogether and using someone's name over and over. It can help you eaaaaaaaase into it, then you can sprinkle in a *they* when you start to feel your "sea legs."

Hey, Mom, you should call Stuart. I know Stuart would love to hear from you. I bet Stuart had an awesome day. *They* were going to shred and get ice cream.

When I see people using this "on-ramp," I think, *Whatever helps—go for it.*

Also, a cute real story:

A friend told their parents they wanted to use *they/them* pronouns. The parents were nervous but supportive and also had just gotten a new cat, so they thought, *Why not have the cat use they/them pronouns too! That way, we can practice without hurting anyone's feelings.*

Moral of all this: Practice makes perfect. And those parents are cute. So is the cat.

If someone is confused about who you're referring to, they'll literally ask. Just be there for the questions, and next time, maybe they won't need so much explanation.

And now, the question buried inside of all of us, the question that keeps some of us from even trying to use *they* in the first place . . .

The feeling,

    the moment . . .

WHAT DO I DO
IF I MESS UP?

(Or: How to recover quickly and respectfully from a slip in gender or name.)

Truth: The magic is in what you do *after* you mess up.

See, there was a misgender moment, but with such a quick fix, there's just one blip and we're back. Let's see it again:

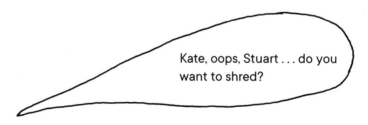

(Duh, I want to shred.)

Why is it important to just correct yourself quickly and move on?

Well, here's the other way people do it:

She's—oops, oh, it's Stuart, not *she*.

Stuart. *They*, I know it's *they*. I am so sorry.

Why did I just do that, I'm so stupid, I can't believe I did that,

I'm such a piece of hot garbage.

Can you ever forgive me, Stuart? Can you? I'm so sorry.

One, what were you even talking about? Do you even remember? All that shame, and we've lost the convo. And tons of energy.

And two, it's an honest mistake that happens to all of us. But when you focus on how bad *you* feel, that moment then becomes about *you* and *your shame feelings* and not about the *they*-using friend just trying to live, just trying to be seen.

So my biggest piece of advice for when you mess up: Correct yourself quickly and just keep going; don't belabor the mistake.

Fix it*
and move on.
Let life
keep living.

*Also, for bonus points, when someone corrects your misgendering or wrong-name moment, instead of saying *sorry*, try saying *thanks*, then move on. That gratitude acknowledges their labor.

Remember, if you get too flustered (or too self-blaming), you're also setting a precedent that might discourage someone from correcting you about their pronouns in the future.

But guess what! Everyone messes up. (Even me!) Just correct and move on.

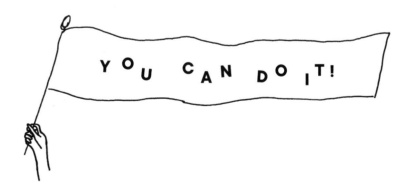

How to Follow Up

If you make a mistake, you can also take your friend aside after the conversation is over, when it's just the two of you, and say something like:

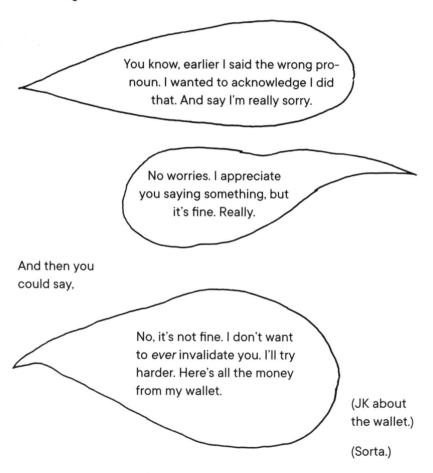

You know, earlier I said the wrong pronoun. I wanted to acknowledge I did that. And say I'm really sorry.

No worries. I appreciate you saying something, but it's fine. Really.

And then you could say,

No, it's not fine. I don't want to *ever* invalidate you. I'll try harder. Here's all the money from my wallet.

(JK about the wallet.)

(Sorta.)

How to Support *They*-Using Buds

When you are in groups of people and you hear someone saying something incorrect—like, an inaccurate theory about trans people, or maybe misgendering or using the wrong name for someone, and nobody else in the room corrects it—you could speak up. It could be the moment of education that saves someone else from having to do that work later.

It's more important now than ever to speak up, say something, and not allow blatant transphobia to happen in your airspace.

Daddy's got this.

How to Show Your Love

There's a lot going on, especially in America, in terms of transgender rights being obliterated.

Like "transgender" being removed federally as a protected class for discrimination, our right to use the bathroom without having to show our junk to prove we're allowed to pee there (this is real), hate crimes, our right to serve in the armed forces . . . Right now, the attempted erasure of trans people is happening everywhere. Let's let the world know we don't want trans people to go anywhere.

Vote.

Sign petitions.

Speak out.

And stop the trans erasure.

Let's do it with love.

We need love in all the ways, but sometimes the best thing an ally can do for us is to say the words we are used to saying over and over . . . to just give us a break.

My sister explains *they* to people left and right, when people say things like:

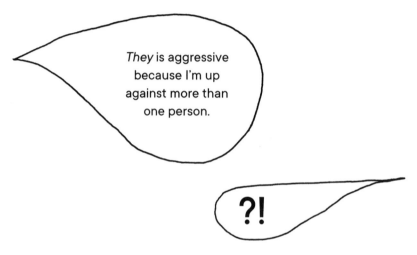

They is aggressive because I'm up against more than one person.

?!

I'm so grateful she has this convo so I don't have to. Who even says that?

But, I mean, maybe I identify as "a hundred dads" and that's why I use they?

More Q's I've legit been asked. So no shame if you also have questions.

Q

Is *they* new?

A:

Thinking of *they* as "new" would erase the existence of many non-Western/BIPOC (Black, indigenous, people of color) cultures that have had—or still do have—similar words to *they* that have existed since the beginning of language. The concept of a gender-neutral identity isn't new. There are many diverse voices across the globe, spanning generations, with similar identifications.

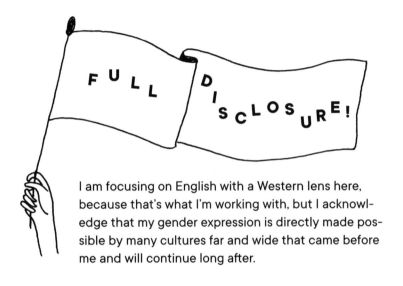

I am focusing on English with a Western lens here, because that's what I'm working with, but I acknowledge that my gender expression is directly made possible by many cultures far and wide that came before me and will continue long after.

Akava'ine
Baklâ
Bissu
Fa'afafine
Hen
Hijra
Kathoey
Khanith
Koekchuch
Māhū
Muxe
Two-spirit
Winkte

And so on and on. This is not a full list but here to illustrate:

This is not new. It's not white. And it's not going anywhere.

Akava'ine: Cook Islands Māori (New Zealand indigenous people) term for third gender. It also means "transgender female" to some.

Baklâ: Philippine word for third gender. Before colonialism, baklâ were revered as spiritual leaders.

Bissu: The *bissu* belong to one of the five genders of the Bugis people, the largest of the three major ethnic groups of South Sulawesi, Indonesia. For one to be considered *bissu*, all aspects of gender must be combined to form a whole.

Fa'afafine: People who identify as having a third gender or nonbinary role in Samoa, American Samoa, and the Samoan diaspora. An estimated 1 to 5 percent of Samoans are *fa'afafine*.

Hen: Added to the most authoritative Swedish language dictionary as a gender-neutral pronoun in 2014. It also shows up in legal documents in Sweden and Finland.

Hijra: A Hindustani word traditionally translated into English as "eunuch" (dudes who lose their junk to be spiritual leaders), but as of a 2014 ruling, hijra has been defined as a third gender and is recognized on official documents in India.

Kathoey: A significant number of Thais perceive *kathoey* as belonging to a third sex. Earlier usage mostly meant "trans woman" but has evolved.

Khanith: A specific third gender category in the Arabian Peninsula.

Koekchuch: A long-gone-from-this-world gender identity in Siberia. AMAB individuals who lived as women during the eighteenth century and early nineteenth century.

Māhū: In Kanaka Maoli (Hawaiian) and Maohi (Tahitian) languages, the word means "in the middle" and refers to third-gender people who fulfill traditional spiritual and social roles in these cultures.

Muxe: A person in Zapotec cultures of Oaxaca seen as a third gender. Includes trans women and those who identify as neither male nor female.

Two-spirit: A modern umbrella term used by some Indigenous North Americans to describe Native people in their communities who fulfill a traditional third-gender (or gender-variant) ceremonial role in their cultures.

Winkte: Lakota shortening of *winyanktehca*, meaning "[wants] to be like a woman" or "two souls person." Though it's used now to refer mostly to homosexual men, many modern *winkte* also participate in the pan-Indian two-spirit community. Seen as a third gender, *winkte* were historically considered sacred. They sometimes participated in naming ceremonies, where their naming of a child was said to bring that child good luck.

Q:

How do you respond to someone saying,
"You're in the wrong bathroom"?

A:

Technically, I *am* in the wrong bathroom.
You know, if it's not gender neutral.

If it is, it's usually a one-holer,
and then I'm asking that someone,

"Are you a boy or a girl?" for me gets a big: "Nope." Neither. In the middle. Between. Beyond. I don't know—all of it.

And if the world isn't able to offer a gender-neutral option, then I'm in the one with a dress on it, and that gets people asking, "But wait . . . *ladies*' room, *girl* talk, so . . . can I use *she* for you?"

Then we give each other that sheepish closemouthed smile, and I have to reiterate:

"Nope.

Not a *she*.

Just here to pee.

It's *they*, thanks."

Sometimes I go in the men's room because sometimes it feels better.

More under the radar. And in some parts of some towns, it feels safer.

But most of the time, honestly, I go wherever smells the best.

Q:

Are most people who use *they/them* pronouns nonbinary or gender nonconforming?

A:

Yes, most people who use *they/them* pronouns identify as nonbinary (a.k.a. enby) or gender-neutral— or rather, neither man nor woman. (Some agender people also use *they*.)

Also, some people who identify as nonbinary and gender neutral don't use *they*. They might use *she* or *he*. Or maybe something different. (As always, just ask. *Kindly*.)

I also have some cis female friends who use *they* because they feel like the constraints of *she* can be ugly—in America specifically. And I know others who use it just so people will hear *they* more.

But most of the time, if they're using *they*, then yes, they're enby. See, you're now hip to gender slang. Enby all you can be.

Q:

Does using *they* mean you're just on your way to transitioning to be a man?

A:

Nope. I never want to be a man. (No offense.)
I'm trans but not transitioning. I'm not changing
anything about myself. I am just me.
But still trans. And genderqueer.

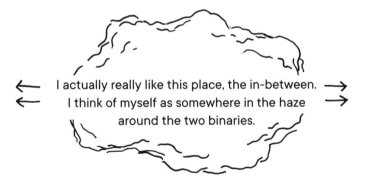

I actually really like this place, the in-between.
I think of myself as somewhere in the haze
around the two binaries.

Growing up, I never felt like a little girl or little boy, and the word *tomboy* felt good, for a while, because it's a bit of a hybrid. Then I was a lesbian, a butch, then along that journey, I found *they*, and gasped:

This is me now. This is me.

I'm here.

I'm genderqueer.

Get used to it.

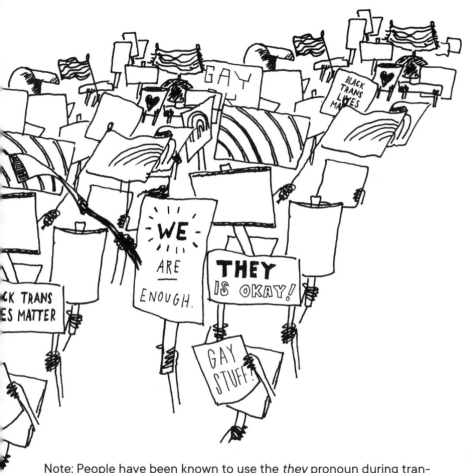

Note: People have been known to use the *they* pronoun during transition. But that's *pretty* rare. It's great to ask. I'll probably repeat that a lot. Just ask.

I asked my GNC/trans friends, "Do you ever *not* like it when people ask your pronouns?"

Most said, "Ask me anytime! We love pronouns!"

But some people did tell me that they've had experiences where nobody is asked their pronoun, then they walk in, and as a "different-looking person," it's all of the sudden:

Hey, everyone! It's pronoun time!

This singles out that "different-looking person" as the only reason to have a conversation about pronouns. Assumptions are still being made. So, yeah. Not great.

I've also heard some queers say, "I just don't like it."

Pronouns, and conversations about pronouns, are just not for them. That's cool too.

We are all humans

and all different.

My openness to pronouns isn't shared by everyone.

But the majority of my GNC/trans friends do feel strongly about creating a world where everyone feels comfortable talking about pronouns and nobody makes assumptions about people.

Q:

How does using gendered language work when joking around? For example, if you're like "girl, pleeeeaase" or "boi, bye," does this offend gender nonconforming people?

A:

For me, it's actually all in the delivery, the intent, who the person saying it to me is, and what our relationship looks like. And though I basically give every queer person a free pass, it's a case-by-case thing. If I know we have love and you don't actually think I'm a GRRRRRL, most likely I'll just "Grrrrrl" you right back. Literally, it's all in the love.

GRRRL

But if you are wondering about gendered language, try out some gender-neutral language and see how it feels. Notice those moments when you default to binary language and see if you can't dream up some other more open ways to greet folks.

Other words to try, instead of . . .

Ladies and gentlemen ⟶ people, peeps, friends, folks, everyone, y'all, you all, fam

Boys and girls ⟶ kids, kiddos, children, friends, angels, rock stars

Sir or ma'am ⟶ you, friend, gentleperson (JK. Sorta.)

Why?

It removes gender, which removes assumptions.

Q:

What are words that replace *niece* and *nephew*? *Aunt* and *uncle*? *Brother, sister*?

A:

I make up words all the time. So do my friends and family. At first, I was Aunkle Stu to my nephews. I'm still Uncle Stu to my friends' kids. And my wife and I joked when we got married that I'd be her *hersband*. Because the word *spouse* just kinda . . . sucks, doesn't it?

My family has the most trouble with this; my mom still reflexively calls me *daughter*, which sounds so funny to me. "My daughter Stuart." I tell her that *child* or *kid*, even *offspring*, would feel better (and, bonus, it sounds like *science*).

While you're at it, try these swaps too!

Mom/Dad	⟶	Parent
Sister/Brother	⟶	Sibling
Grandma/ Grandpa	⟶	Grandparent
Wife/Husband	⟶	Spouse, Partner, Hersband
Son/Daughter	⟶	Child, Kid, Offspring

Nibling is something I've heard and used instead of *niece* or *nephew*. I've heard nonbinary parents go by *Bobo* or *Baba*. I've heard people call their private parts their *trinkets* . . . Honestly, I think it's fun to find what fits, and to choose for ourselves what feels right.

Words are fun. When we start messing with them, we can give power to what we really want this world to look like, all through the language we choose.

You can also rephrase sentences to allow a nonbinary person to not have to wear terms that don't fit.

Sometimes, for a nonbinary person, it's as simple as changing the order and structure, like:

These are my nephews, Finn and Sawyer,

rather than,

I am their, uhhhhh . . .

Honestly, that's a trick queer folks use a lot. It's subtle and unnoticeable.

The gays rephrase.

And here's another trick frequented in queer circles: the magic of the phrase *that person*.

Let's try it out.

Think of something that happened, like: Sam came into your room. OK. Explain to me what happened, but use *this/that person*. Not *Sam*. No pronouns.

That person came into my room with a pizza!

(Aw, Sam. I don't eat cheese.)

When I first heard someone use *that person*, it sounded funny to me too. *That person. This person.* How informal, right?

Nah. Now, I love hearing this. It makes no assumptions. It holds the space open. And you might not ever even notice it, but trans and non-binary people do—we see *that person* as a clue to know we're safe.

That person.

So, essentially, the

HOT TAKE:

BE

THAT

PERSON.

Q:

Who should I ask for their pronouns?

A:

With adults, do it all the time. Make it a thing. In my queer community, it's really not a big deal anymore. It's not even that radical. Yes, it took some years, but you, too, can be a part of this movement. Ask your mom. Ask your spouse. Ask the person beep-beeping your groceries, if it feels right. Why not make it something that everyone is just always doing, so when it comes to me having to have *that* conversation, everyone already knows how to do it. That's a world I'd be into. By asking, and not assuming, it also means you're no longer gender-clocking people, and you know what I said about gender-clocking.

(Don't do it.)

Q:

How do I ask someone's pronouns?

A:

Open up your mouth and say,

WHAT ARE YOUR PRONOUNS?

Don't offer a caveat. Don't start with, "I am not sure I should be asking this . . ." Just let it rip. Cis people show the privilege of never having to say their own pronouns by exhibiting immense discomfort around starting the conversation in the first place. (Cis fragility?)

That's not my life. I pronoun talk all the time.

Q:

When do I ask someone's pronouns?

A:

You might be talking to someone, wondering if you should ask about pronouns because they look like they might be a *they* user, but you don't want to assume. And then you ask yourself *when* you should pipe up about your curiosity about pronouns.

Personally, I'm like, let's get this done ASAP. I know what I look like, I know I make people wonder, and I'd love to just get the pronoun moment handled so we can move along with our lives. Just, you know, watch out for any assumptions.

For kiddos, asking/talking about pronouns can be different.

Kids might still be figuring their gender stuff out, and a pronoun circle where all eyes are on them and their ever-changing bodies—

it just might not feel good.

Here are some tips for handling it a tad differently with our younger ones.

For Teachers: How to Do Pronouns Better

(Or for anyone who interacts with young people)

- Kids may still be in the process of figuring things out. In fact, maybe we all are. But especially before college age, the question, "What's your pronoun?" might actually elicit tears.

- Why? Maybe they are transgender and wanting to *pass*, and you asking makes them feel like they don't signal the right pronoun to the world.

- Or maybe they just don't know yet and are on a journey of discovery, not at a place to share just yet, and the pressure of identifying is too much.

- These are all valid experiences that should be honored.

Be aware that all school settings may not be a safe space to share.

Bullying is still a thing. Kids can be mean.

Pronoun circles may also not work so great for: shy ones, people who don't "look" GNC, and people who are not out publicly yet.

You can optionally share pronouns when exchanging names or using name tags, but always give people a way to opt out.

Don't single out a GNC person in public if you don't need to, including asking them their pronoun and gender identity in large groups. Watch for how their friends refer to them or how they refer to themselves.

Ask privately, in a very neutral way. Like, in conversation, as the need for pronouns comes up. Kids say they prefer to have this convo one-on-one.

Q:

How do we teach children to use *they/them*?

A:

You'd be surprised. Kids will probably teach *us* a few things. They basically come out at birth without a gender or any concept of it. And then they learn through their families, schools, and stuff they watch that the world divides people into two genders, two pronouns, *he* and *she*, blue and pink, strong and weak. And they absorb it and pass it on. Kids are born fluid; it's our world that boxes them in.

Some kids experience their gender as a meandering road as they find themselves moving back and forth along the spectrum and beyond, and sometimes *they* can be a healing place of refuge for them.

So why not teach them about *they* when you're teaching them other pronouns?

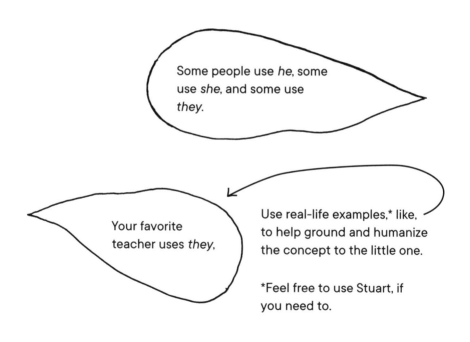

Some people use *he*, some use *she*, and some use *they*.

Your favorite teacher uses *they*,

Use real-life examples,* like, to help ground and humanize the concept to the little one.

*Feel free to use Stuart, if you need to.

How to Talk to Kids about Pronouns

A script

Hi, _____. I love when we talk to each other. It makes
    _{NAME}
me feel _____.
    _{FEELING}

Do you know the words *she* and *he*?

(WAIT FOR THEIR ANSWER. IF IT'S NO, EXPLAIN.)

He and *she* are pronouns, or generic words people use as a
way to not use names over and over again. Boys and men
use *he*, and girls and women use *she*. Do you know what your
pronoun is? (DISCUSS THEIR ANSWER.)

Did you know some people use the pronoun *they* instead of
he or *she*? Do you know why? It's because they don't think of
themselves as a boy or a girl. Do we know anyone like that?
(DISCUSS.)

They is for everyone between and beyond.

You can tell me if you want to use any of these words to describe you. Or not.

I'm here to listen at any time, whatever you want to tell me. Any questions?

(LISTEN TO THEIR QUESTIONS AND ANSWER THE BEST YOU CAN.)

I love you.

Q:

Any tips for parents of kids who use *they/them*?

A:

First off, yay. If they're *theying*, you're yaying . . . as a parent. You're doing great already. Just remember, upcoming generations are changing every definition. Especially with words about gender. And this is only the beginning.

You holding your child's identity as valid and beautiful—*that is the future*.

So, thank you.

Things to do:

1. **Be patient.** It's a wild ride to find one's own self. Buckle up. (Your love is safety.)

2. **Listen.** Ask questions and stay curious but really try to *hear* your child. Vulnerability is powerful in its expression. So be brave and tell your child they are brave when they share with you.

3. **Believe them.** Your child's truth is theirs and theirs alone. Trust that they know who they are.

Some other stuff to think about
(when being a thoughtful parent):

- **Give gender-free gifts:** And clue your whole family in to the presence of their presents.

- **If family members can't abide,** don't make your child do a public gift opening. It can be crushing for a kid to open a card that says, "To my grandson," when that's not how they feel about their body and life.

- **Talk the talk:** Have the awkward conversations with other family members and draw boundaries so your kid doesn't have to. (They're just a kid.)

- **Ask them:** Always check in about what they want other people to know.

- **Thank them:** It's brave to share this stuff with anyone, let alone your parents.

Q:

If we move toward a world where things aren't gendered, will we still have transgender people?

A:

Honestly, I hope we all transcend gender.

But to answer perhaps the underlying question: If we stop caring about gender, can we all forget about hormone therapy and gender-affirmation surgeries?

Probably not. No.

But I don't know. I can't speak for those who are on that path, and I don't know where this world is going.
That said . . .

I think

transgender and nonbinary people

have existed

forever,

and I believe

we are sacred and beautiful and will always be here.

As a demographic, we have historically had to fight against our erasure almost nonstop, and yet—we are still here.

We will always be here.

Do's and Don'ts of *Theying* a *They*

ask pronouns.

DN'T

call them "preferred pronouns." Sure, we *prefer* you call us by them, but it's not like we prefer a gender, we just *are* one. Dig?

put pronouns on name tags and email signatures.

D N'T

avoid pronoun talk in places where genderqueer people are
absent. If it feels safe to talk about pronouns and gender when a
GNC/nonbinary person is not in the room, think of how
dope we will feel when we are!

support your friends safely coming out and becoming their most authentic selves. Yay!

D⊖N'T

out someone without permission. You need to check in first to make sure sensitive information can be shared before telling anyone anything. It's cute that you wanna yell it from the rooftops, but sadly, it's still not safe for trans folks everywhere. Until we are safe everywhere, keep the outing inside.

D

help us fight for trans rights in bathrooms. (When there are bills on ballots and policies at organizations that equate trans people in bathrooms to sexual predators, and then there's a marked increase in hate crimes *against trans people* in and around bathrooms, well, we need everyone's help. Your voice, your vote, a sign in your yard—it all helps to fight this monster.)

D⊙N'T

pee on the seat-y. If you do, be a sweetie. Clean it up.

Part Three:
The Fun Stuff

(and Some Not-Fun Stuff)

The Holy Gay Acronym

What letter are we adding next?

Sure, it's a joke among us, but it's beautiful, if you think about it: we, the holy gay community, are so into inclusion and openness that the letters just keep a-coming . . .

First, they called us

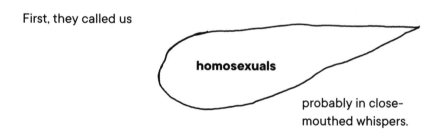

homosexuals

probably in close-mouthed whispers.

Then, it was just

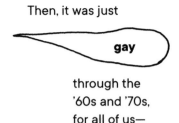

gay

through the
'60s and '70s,
for all of us—

or

queer

but only as a slur. Back then, being
queer was considered a mental
illness (until the American Psychiat-
ric Association removed it from their
manual in 1973), and it was
very scary and misunderstood.

Then we were

gay and lesbian

to signify that women were also part of the community.

And the word *gay* started to mean specifically "man-on-man stuff." As
the fight for civil rights blazed on, queers knew unity would be important in moving the status quo. But coming together definitely did not
come easy.

Then, in the mid-to-late–80s, it was

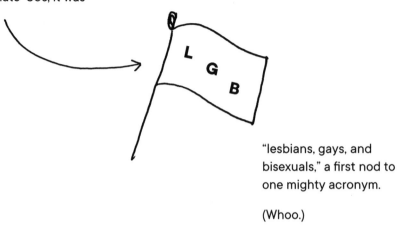

"lesbians, gays, and bisexuals," a first nod to one mighty acronym.

(Whoo.)

I've heard the *L* comes first because men wanted to acknowledge their privilege and allow their scissor sisters this honor. Nice work.

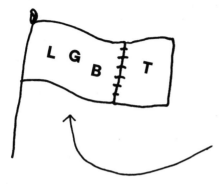

hit the scene in the '90s to include *T* for "transgender."

Adding this *T* broke the construct of the acronym. At first, it was only about sexual orientation (lesbian, gay, bisexual), but now, gender identity was included as well. We were growing.

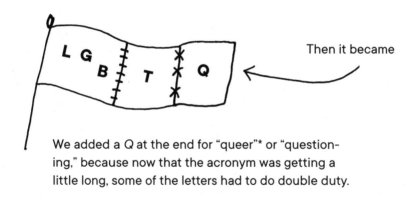

Then it became

We added a Q at the end for "queer"* or "questioning," because now that the acronym was getting a little long, some of the letters had to do double duty.

*About the word *queer*. My mom asked me one time, very timidly, "But isn't that, like, a slur . . . against you?"

QUEER

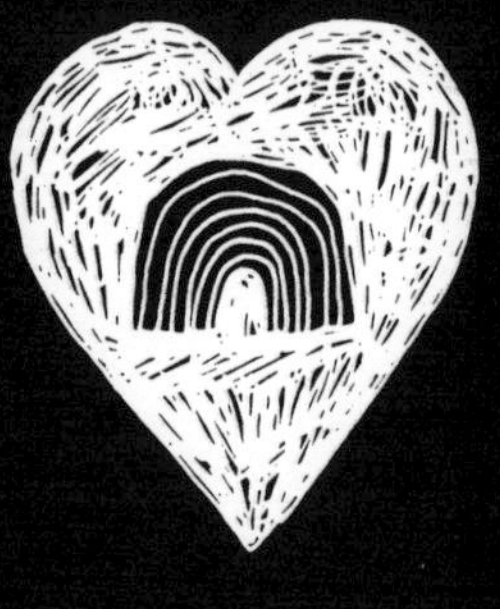

Queer is such a special word to me, and to so many in my community, because it calls for an openness of identity; anyone can identify as just queer, no labels beyond that. No binaries. Nothing you have to claim forever. No "team" you're on.

Queer means anything and everything that's not heterosexual, and that's a wide space of opportunity for identity and love. And we rock it.

The word *queer* is a badge of courage, because it is still a fight. Many of us have reclaimed that word, that slur, all the slurs, really—*dyke, fag, homo*. We grabbed all that we could to take the power back. Now we call each other by these words. We put them on shirts and flags and banners. So when they are used against us (and yes, they still are sometimes), it doesn't hurt as much.

Because, yeah,

I am a
dyke

and a
faggot.*

So what, big whoop.

(It's also good to note that some people of the **LGBTQ+** persuasion absolutely hate the word *queer*, and that is their right too. To each their own.)

*And please remember: these words are still considered slurs unless you are a dyke or faggot yourself.

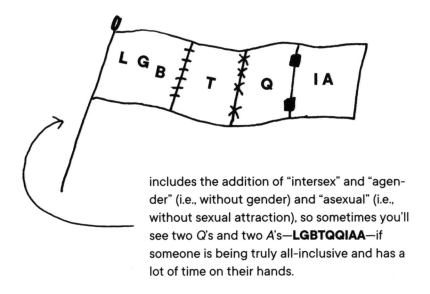

includes the addition of "intersex" and "agender" (i.e., without gender) and "asexual" (i.e., without sexual attraction), so sometimes you'll see two Q's and two A's—**LGBTQQIAA**—if someone is being truly all-inclusive and has a lot of time on their hands.

Oftentimes, these days, you might also see a *P* for "pansexual," like so:

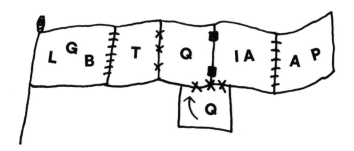

Wow, I'm getting tired just writing that. (I have yet to see an *O* for "omnisexual." Have you?)

But the latest and greatest I've seen is:

2 S L G B T +

This acronym starts with *2S* to signify "two-spirit," the term used by some indigenous North American people in their communities for people who exist as third gender or gender variant.

And that plus sign at the end there lets you know it's all in there—the *Q*'s, the *P*'s, the *I*'s, the *A*'s. They're all under our umbrella

(*ella, ella, aye, aye, aye*).

And if you have even more letters for us, we're ready for 'em.

Because we *are* family. We keep growing. And so does that acronym.

Great Moments in *They* History

Interestingly enough, if we look way back when, before any of us were alive, we'll find a lot more fluidity in gender expression.

Think about Ancient Greek times: men wore dresses and had a lot of sex with men. Like, *a lot*. But there was no concept of homosexuality yet, so Ancient Greek men were considered no less of a man for having another man get all up in their pants (so to speak—remember, they weren't wearing pants; they wore long, flowy dress-type things). Men were as gay as damn parades without having to call it that or have a parade.

Women, unfortunately, seem to have been subjugated from day one and made to wear all kinds of extremely uncomfortable outfits at different periods of time. Lesbian stuff was happening, of course, but it was way more hidden. Or, because of patriarchy, we never heard about it.

Then, basically, Christianity happened. (We could have a whole book just on that.) And in the nineteenth century, during the process of medicalizing sexuality, Western society decided that we needed to make a "scientific" binary system of female and male.

So, we did.

And, wow, was that a

SLIPPERY

We based the binary on genitals and clothing preference and gender roles. Then pink and blue became a thing.

Think about this: In the 1800s, all children wore frilly white dresses. And in early twentieth century, the gendered colors were flip-flopped: pink was for boys and blue was for girls. According to *Ladies Home Journal*, in 1918, boys were "appropriately dressed" wearing pink because it was a "more strong and decided color," while blue was "daintier, perfect for girls."

Just goes to show that even our gendered color choices are a product of socialization.

SLOPE.

Cute story:

When I was born, I was small—five pounds something—
and neither of the hospital-issued pink or blue hats
would fit me. So my mom and a nurse got creative and
found a nylon (like, a pair of tights) and cut the end off.

It fit perfectly.

Not pink, not blue, but tan.

Control top.

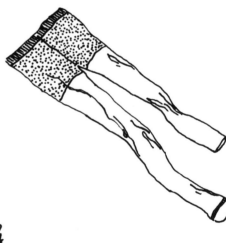

Ha. See. I was born this *they*.

Studies say that boys and girls are both born with basically the same brain but then are socialized differently. Children then mimic the gendered personality and the gender expression they are taught and see (like goatees, skirts, fingerless gloves, tutus, capes, Hammer pants).

During the 1940s in the United States, a major shift happened: pink was feminized, and it also took on a meaning of "weaker or less than," and blue was for boys, and meant "strong." Then, in the '50s, the rigidity of gender and the assigned colors perfectly reflected the control people of the time wanted in their homes and work.

Women were expected to stay in the kitchen, and men were out working or drinking and smoking.

And society drew very clear lines around what it meant to be a man and what it meant to be a woman, dictating what people could and could not wear, or say, or even what jobs a person could hold.

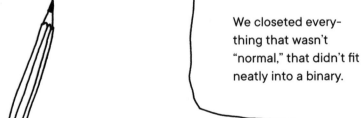

We closeted everything that wasn't "normal," that didn't fit neatly into a binary.

And that repression—like anything that attempts to hide something that exists and has existed since the beginning of time—leads to expression. Gender expression is only a big deal right now because it's coming after many centuries of repression. A shift happened in the '60s, and now here we are again

in an explosion of freeness.

And I feel so grateful. What a time to be alive.

The Timeline

They is just the iteration right now of this gender expression. But there is a long, long history of gender neutrality and pronoun exploration.

Sometime between 1350 and 1360

"William," a poet, translates *The Romance of William and the Werewolf* into Middle English, using a singular *they* pronoun to keep their identity secret.

1594

William Shakespeare writes *The Comedy of Errors*, later to be published in 1623, and includes the line: "There's a man I meet but doth salute me. As if I were their well-acquainted friend."

1792

Scottish economist James Anderson advocates for *ou* as a pronoun without gender. Gender-free pronouns since the 1700s, people. *Wow.*

1808

Samuel Taylor Coleridge, the poet, wrote in his notebooks: "whether we may not, nay ought not, to use a neutral pronoun relative . . . to the word 'Person' . . . in order to avoid particularising man or woman, or in order to express sex indifferently?"

Coleridge suggested using *it* and *which* as ungendered pronouns instead of *he*, *she*, *him*, *her*, *who*, and *whom*. Pretty advanced for 1808.

1858

Charles Crozat Converse coins *thon* as a gender-neutral pronoun. (It doesn't catch on.)

1850

The Interpretation Act 1850, known to its haters as the Generic He law, is signed in by UK Parliament, basically saying that the pronoun *he* can stand for "he or she." Cool. (Not.)

1900

An article in the *Baltimore Sun* calls for the creation of a third gender for, and I quote, "manly women and womanly men."

lol. But, OK, I mean, I guess it was ahead of the times.

1881

Emily Dickinson uses singular *they* in a letter. She sends it.

Twentieth Century

Legalese, a.k.a. the words on law contracts and documents, adopts a singular *they* so as not to have to change *he/she*, *his/her* pronouns on every document, and it is still commonly, although not universally, used.

1970s

Mx, pronounced "mix," hits the scene as an alternative to *Mr./Ms./Mrs.*

1985

Mx is used more widely among writers, activists, and people who know what's up.

1981

The Handbook of Nonsexist Writing calls for the abolishment of the "generic he."

Stuart Getty is born on August 17. Thanks, Mom.

1998

The *New Oxford Dictionary of English* accepts singular *they* and uses it in definitions.

1996

The New Fowler's Dictionary of Modern English Usage calls the trend of using singular *they* "irreversible."

Duh.

2017

The gender marker *X* shows up on more states' driver's licenses. As of 2020, *X* is available in seventeen states.

The Chicago Manual of Style and the *AP Stylebook* accept singular *they* as a gender-neutral pronoun.

Gender options beyond *M* and *F* populate more and more drop-down menus.

2015

They is voted Word of the Year by the American Dialect Society (and is declared their Word of the Decade in 2019).

2016

Oregon is the first state to rule in favor of allowing for *X* gender markers (for nonbinary identity) on driver's licenses.

2018

The Netherlands issues the world's first gender-neutral passport.

2019

Merriam-Webster adds the nonbinary *they* pronoun to their dictionary and names it their Word of the Year.

Dot, dot, dot.

The world is changing, and history is being made all the time.

It's all just going to keep evolving, and we, the *theys*,
aren't going anywhere.

Promise.

DeLorean.
(Time is not linear.
Neither is sexuality.)

Queerbook

Famous people doing cool genderqueer things

Alok Vaid-Menon, *gender nonconforming, they*

• Writer, poet, performance artist, activist

• Featured on HBO, MTV, *The Guardian*, *National Geographic*, the *New York Times*, and the *New Yorker* and appeared as themself on *Random Acts of Flyness* in 2018

• Part of DarkMatter, a South Asian transgender performance poetry group

• Known for trans activism and biting satire within their performances

"We have been taught to fear the very things that have the potential to set us free."

Asia Kate Dillon, *nonbinary, they*

- Played first nonbinary character on mainstream North American TV

- Breakout role as hedge-fund intern Taylor in *Billions*

- Started removing gendered pronouns from their bios in 2015

"Anyone who has gone on a journey of self-discovery with specific regard to either their gender identity or their sexual orientation, I think has had to look at themselves from sort of every angle."

Jacob Tobia, *genderqueer, they*

- Writer, LGBTQ+ activist

- Known best for their memoir, *Sissy: A Coming-of-Gender Story*

- Published an essay on MTV about being genderqueer

"I'm a genderqueer person who was assigned male at birth and likes to rock high heels and lipstick, but in the current moment of visibility for transgender women and men, very few people can seem to get my identity right."

Jonathan Van Ness, *gender nonconforming, they/he**

• Hair magician and star of *Queer Eye*

• Popularized the phrase, "Can you even believe?"

• Wears heels like an absolute pro

"Any opportunities I have to break down stereotypes of the binary, I am down for it. I'm here for it."

*JVN accepts both *he* and *they* as valid pronouns.

Sam Smith, *genderqueer, they*

• English singer, songwriter

• Rose to fame after being featured in a single by Disclosure, "Latch"

• Came out as gay in 2014, then as genderqueer in 2017

• Hot, croon-y angel

"I don't know what the title would be, but I feel just as much a woman as I am man."

Ser Anzoategui, *nonbinary, they*

• Latinx/Chicanx actor, playwright, artivist

• Breakout role on *East Los High*

• Best known as Eddy, sensitive, butch widow on *Vida*

• Activist fighting against the gentrification of East LA

"Don't call me an actress. In fact, let's get rid of that title altogether."

Thank you, famous bbs, for showing up and being you.

You're helping make the world a better place.

Things That Suck for GNC Folks

Just a few things that could definitely get better for us gender-creative types.

The TSA

Honestly—the TSA is at the top of my list. TSA scanners are actually a really flawed, transphobic system for your trans and nonbinary friends.

Did you know that when you step into a full-body scanner, a TSA agent presses a pink or blue button to gender-clock you based on your gender presentation? Seriously.

(I asked some TSA agents why they do this, and they said, "People have different places they can put things . . . We're scanning orifices.")

Ever wonder why so many genderqueer and trans folks are getting the back-of-the-hand-pat-down treatment at airports? Now you know. The TSA can't figure out our orifices.

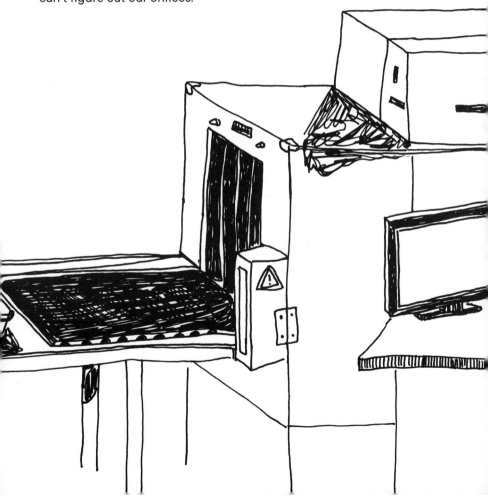

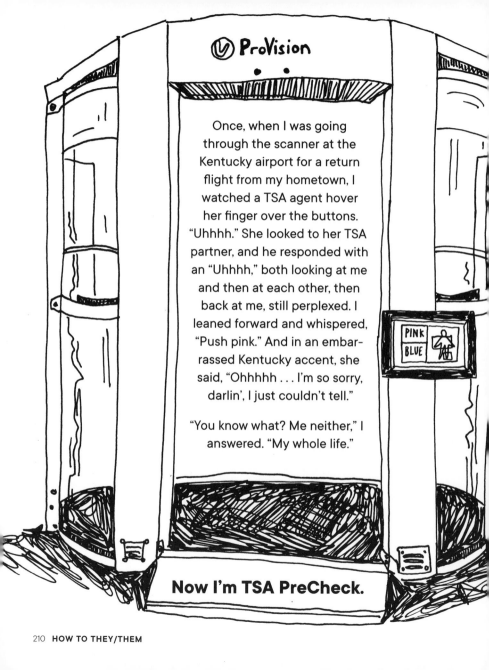

(V) ProVision

Once, when I was going through the scanner at the Kentucky airport for a return flight from my hometown, I watched a TSA agent hover her finger over the buttons. "Uhhhh." She looked to her TSA partner, and he responded with an "Uhhhh," both looking at me and then at each other, then back at me, still perplexed. I leaned forward and whispered, "Push pink." And in an embarrassed Kentucky accent, she said, "Ohhhhh . . . I'm so sorry, darlin', I just couldn't tell."

"You know what? Me neither," I answered. "My whole life."

PINK
BLUE

Now I'm TSA PreCheck.

Every Form Ever

I feel like a broken record, but official forms and drop-down menus are what's actually broken. Someone is writing that code. Someone is designing those forms. And if you know who they are, show them this page.

I am noticing more and more sign-in, enrollment, submission, and online systems opening up their gender options, not just listing *Male* and *Female*, and it's making me smile. It's becoming more common, but it's not everywhere. We still have work to do.

If you are the one crafting an online or paper form for your organization or company, ask yourself and your establishment: Are you using a binary when you don't need to be?

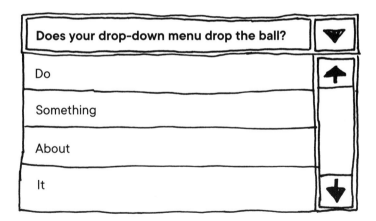

(OK. I'll drop it.)

Legal Names at Doctor's Offices

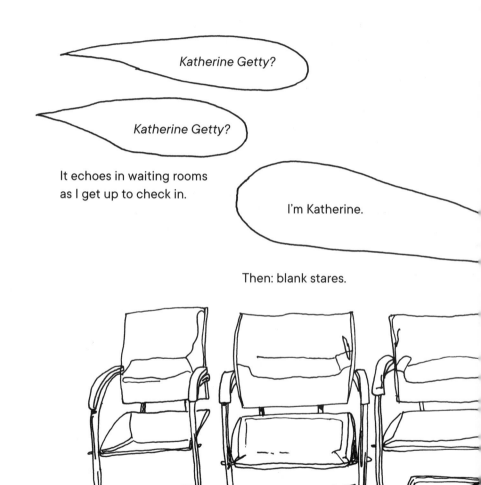

Katherine Getty?

Katherine Getty?

It echoes in waiting rooms
as I get up to check in.

I'm Katherine.

Then: blank stares.

Their brains: *Wait, you're a man. Wait, do men ever go by "Katherine"?*

I have been to Planned Parenthoods and a few other practitioners who address me as Stuart Getty. Even if my legal name has to be used on every test tube and official form, I never have to see the name I don't like. But these interactions are rare. Most of the time, I just have to grin and bear it as I get Katherine'd* and *she*'d and then stuffed into a crinkly white robe.

*Katherine is my "**deadname,**" a term used to define the birth name of someone who no longer goes by that. Dead means we killed that name in our circles, but not everyone does this! So ask around, but tread lightly with the dead . . . names. RIP Kathy. Stuart's alive!

The possible-worst is when they list the name

Katherine "Stuart" Getty

**on forms, with my name in quotes
like some alias or joke.**

Making me still look at that Katherine and feel *Stuart*
invalidated by those quotes.

I just hope that someone in the medical field reads this and it helps change some system.

Because it just doesn't have to be this way.

Does it?

I know insurance relies on a "birth name" system, but I wonder: Why do some offices go that extra step for gender-variant people and others don't?

Doctors, you tell me.

Hmm, do you know what else sucks?

Family functions with
"relatives who don't get it"
in attendance.

Restaurant servers who say,
"Hey, ladies."

Filling up at a gas
station alone in a
city that's not a city.

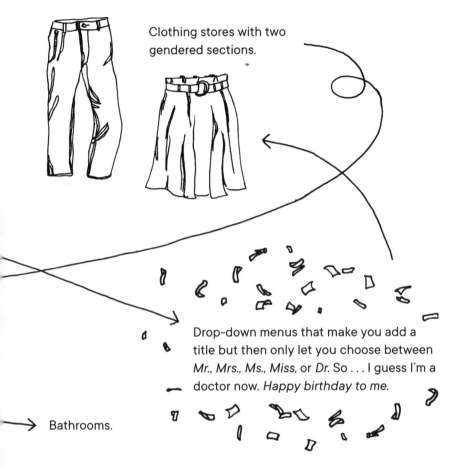

Clothing stores with two gendered sections.

Drop-down menus that make you add a title but then only let you choose between *Mr., Mrs., Ms., Miss,* or *Dr.* So . . . I guess I'm a doctor now. *Happy birthday to me.*

Bathrooms.

Our society is so much better than it ever has been for gender-neutral identities, but just ask yourself: What still needs to change? How can we all help to create a better world for the next generation?

What things do *you* want to change?

Cis Moment

Wait just one moment—what's all this have to do with cis people?

By using and acknowledging *they*, we help challenge gender norms and learned social behaviors for everyone, including our friends who use *he* and *she*. Because gender constraints hurt everyone. Gender freedom allows all types of people to express their genders however they feel is right. Just be free. Forget gender norms and choose for yourself how you want to be you.

Let's abolish all the dumb gender tropes:

- Women are considered loud or pushy when being direct or vocal. Or just *bitches*... while men act the same way and are revered for it, especially in business. (Grr.)

- Women should be ladylike. *Women are to be seen, not heard.* I can't even with this.

- Boys don't cry... or rather, men are socialized to not show emotion or any sign of "weakness" when, in fact, sometimes the strongest thing to do is feel things.

- Boys and men are allowed to feel one emotion: anger. Or, you know, arousal. And if a man is ever sad, it must be related to sports or, like, dropping meat in the dirt—not real feelings.

(Boo all this stuff.)

Our world tells us so many things that men and women should and should not do.

Don't

for it.

Let's make toxic masculinity extinct. Let's make the rigidity of femininity a thing of the past. Let's make gender so fluid that anyone can be anything they want to be.

Let's all be rad to one another and let our identities be as expansive as the love in our hearts.

No, *really*.

Sounds cheesy, but that's the true dream.

What to Do If Someone's Using the Wrong Pronouns *on Purpose*

The Ding-Dong Deuce

Step one:

Find (or make) poop.

Step two:

Put poop in paper bag.

Step three:

Place paper bag on steps of hater's house.

Step four:

Light bag on fire.

Step five: Ring doorbell.

Step six:

(Fast.)

They come out, stamp it out, and get poop all over themselves _because transphobia is poo poo._ (Make sure they're home; we're not trying to burn anything down here.)

Just kidding.

I would never suggest such a thing.

It's probably illegal. And, as you know, I'm all about that love.

Here are a few real (legal) things you can do to help encourage people to use the right pronouns and names.

What to Do If Someone's Using the Wrong Pronouns *by Accident, Repeatedly*

Called **the Repetitive Correct**, my saint of a wife does this all the time with my family:

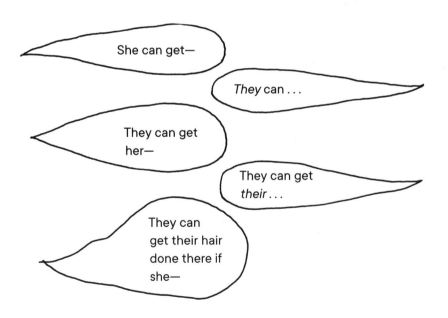

She can get—

They can . . .

They can get her—

They can get *their* . . .

They can get their hair done there if she—

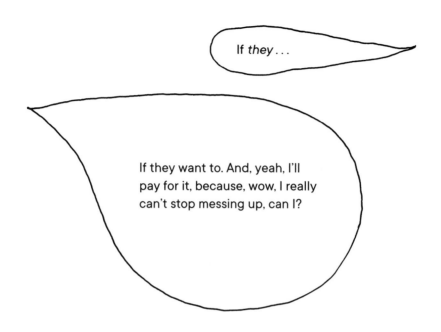

If *they* . . .

If they want to. And, yeah, I'll pay for it, because, wow, I really can't stop messing up, can I?

If you go this route, it can be good to show compassion for those trying and failing, but also for yourself, because the continuous correcting is a lot of work and can be really draining.

Remember to give yourself breaks too. Sometimes, you might just roll your eyes instead.

For my *they*-using bbs:

What to Do If You Use *They* and Are at the End of Your Rope with Loved Ones

You don't necessarily have to sit down for this conversation, but it helps. Tea might help too. Maybe turn your body to face the person you're addressing? Take deep breaths before and during the chat.

1. Talk about what they've done that doesn't work for you, but phrase things in terms of *your* experience and how it makes *you* feel: "I notice myself feeling hurt and disappointed when you misgender me. I know you don't do it on purpose, and it's hard for you, but every time, it just kicks my legs out from under me. Especially when you don't correct yourself after."

2. Use calm, easy language. Own your part of things ("I know I get upset and hard to talk to when it happens . . .") but be direct in what you do not like. And what is not acceptable to you. Know your boundaries. And if they cross them, say it, friend.

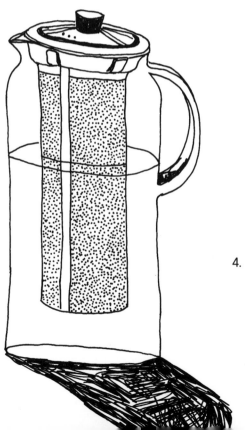

3. Give actionable steps for them to rectify the problematic behavior:

"Next time you misgender me, please make sure you correct yourself in the moment. Or maybe do some practice on your own so it happens less? Maybe read this book by a friend named Stuart?"

4. Take more deep breaths and be sweet to yourself, because, remember, this is work.

A **call in** is the better version of a **callout** (where you just blast some-one and challenge them directly about bad behaviors and then leave them in the dust) because a call in is asking for you to bring empathy and patience to the table. It still calls for change and deems that shit unacceptable. But it's nice about it.

It treats that person like a peer, someone you'd want to stay in community with,

not

just

cancel.

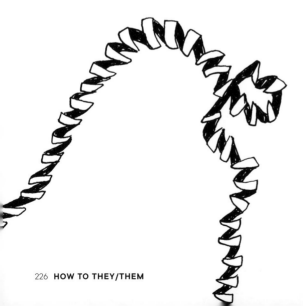

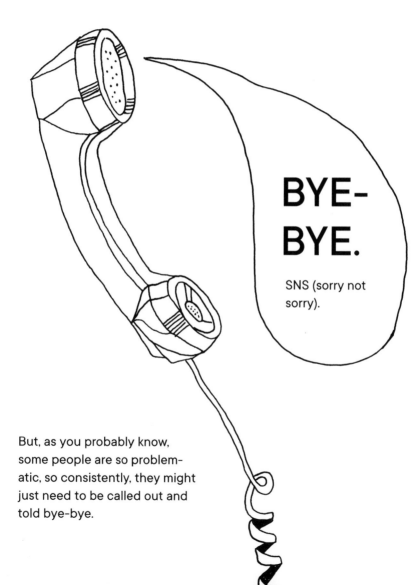

BYE-BYE.

SNS (sorry not sorry).

But, as you probably know, some people are so problematic, so consistently, they might just need to be called out and told bye-bye.

What to Do If You Need to Give an Ultimatum

This one is usually a last-ditch effort. Basically, it's a sit-down call in with an ultimatum finish. But I've also seen it done via text. (Desperate times . . .)

Just like you eventually have to cut off that racist uncle when he won't stop using that word, there is also a line with this. Where is your line? How much can someone misgender, deadname, and invalidate someone before you just have to say goodbye? It's different for all of us.

And I'm here to tell you that, sometimes, it is healthiest to cut people off if they won't change their behavior.

My only tip? Do this with a lot of heart. Because it can be rough.

"So, you've been misgendering me for years now. I always correct you. I say *they* after every *she*. And *child* when you say *daughter*. And *people* when you say *girls*. And you just don't seem to understand how truly painful your words are, just how much they communicate to me, 'I don't see you, the real you.' So I've got to go. It hurts too much. If you can't change, I won't be hanging around you any longer. The invalidation isn't good for my health. I hope you can work to change your ways. I love you."

If this is where you're at, having to cut someone out of your life to stay safe, I'm truly sorry.

I see you. And I know it hurts.

Some Tips for Professionals

When doing business, if diversity is important to you, don't get caught with your they pants down:

- Use gender-neutral terms during all service interactions. Don't *sir* or *ma'am* people. It's not 1954.

- Never assume someone's gender.

- Try not to have only binary bathrooms in your place of business. Or at least change the signage so it's explicit that it's an inclusive restroom.

- Avoid directing people to gendered restrooms. Say, "The bathrooms are right down the hall," rather than, "Your door is on the right," sending them to the women's room or men's room based on your perception of their gender.

- Make sure your biz has pronouns on things like name tags and email signatures and business cards and even signs. And if you use intake forms, provide another box to check besides *M* and *F*. Please? For me?

- When talking about people before you know gender, use singular *they* or avoid pronouns, if you can.

- Write letters and emails without assuming gender, so nix the *Mr.* or *Ms.* unless you know for a fact that's how they identify.

Why is all of this important?

Because we're building a better world for the next generation. Or rather, maybe *they're* the ones building it?

According to a report by trend forecasting agency J. Walter Thompson Innovation Group, more than half the members of Generation Z (those born late-1990s to the early aughts) identify as "not straight": not gay, not bi, not whatever labels or words earlier generations used to define identity. They just shrug, roll their eyes, and say, "Everything's just more fluid than that."

Not straight.

I see so much happening in younger culture to blur the hard lines and labels around sexuality and gender. It's really quite beautiful.

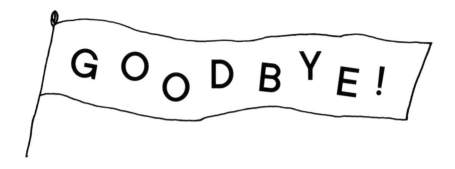

Maybe I'm idealistic, maybe I'm naive, but I do believe all humans are inherently good and judgment free and that—really—everything is love.

(This paper is love. The desk is love. That doorway is love.)

I think we as a society do want to grow to accept more authenticity and expression of identities, because isn't that what all of us want, anyway?

The freedom to be ourselves. And to be loved and accepted just as we are.

Or, you know, *they* are.

Acknowledgments

I'd like to thank my wife, Nora, for believing in me. And all my friends, especially PTalk for telling me, "Daddy's got this," even when I didn't know I did. So much love to Mom, Wayne, Dad, Mary Ann, Liz, Clay, Sarah, Beth, and Drew for being the type of family where I could grow into becoming exactly who I am. Love always to Livi, Grandma Hamblin, and all my ancestors for being with me on this journey. I'd also like to thank my magical communities for the openness in my life made possible by your love. Thank you to my editor Hannah and *Within* magazine, because those two coming together is why this book exists. Thank you to all my English teachers along the way who taught me the rules so I knew just how to break them. And thanks to all of you. Really. Bless up.

Resources

If you or someone you know is having a lot of feelings about their gender, there are places to go, like queer organizations (the SF LGBT Center in the Bay Area, Q Center in Portland, Gay City in Seattle, etc.). I think it's always great to be somewhere other queers are hanging out, to feel validated whatever your identity.

I can't recommend the Trans Lifeline enough. They have a website (TransLifeline.org) and a hotline (1–877–565–8860), so there's always a real person to call and talk to—because I guarantee: you are not alone, you're worth it, and you're enough. Just talk to somebody, anybody, because we want you here. We do.

Some other places to learn more about gender freedom and goodness:

- **ToniLatour.com/hello-there:** An art project by Toni Latour with printable PDF signs that encourage the use of gender-free language in public spaces.

- **HRC.org/resources/parents-for-transgender-equality -national-council:** These parents fight for rights, but they also compile resources to help parents and kids alike.

- **GenderSpectrum.org:** An organization fighting for equality for kids and teens of all gender representations.

- **PFLAG.org:** The old standby, a queer organization that's been around for decades, which stands for "Parents and Family of Lesbians and Gays." And that's just what it is.

- **them.us:** Launched originally by Condé Nast in print, and now online only, it's self-described as "a next-generation community platform . . . all through the lens of today's LGBTQ community."

- **Genderfork.com:** A supportive community and website that explores gender variance through photography, profiles, and discussions.

- **IHeartSingularThey.com:** A bright, colorful, scrolly one-pager-type educational website dedicated to singular *they*.

- **TGIJP.org:** The Transgender Gender-Variant and Intersex Justice Project is a group of transgender, gender-variant, and intersex people—inside and outside of prisons.

Right this very second, more and more entities are being formed to talk about gender and pronouns and all the freedoms we all want to explore. Just google it and feel the truth through the power of the interweb:

You are not alone.